Musings of a
Catastrophic Mind

Musings of a Catastrophic Mind

a collection of poetry and prose

LISA M. LILITH

300 SOUTH MEDIA GROUP

✧

NEW YORK

ISBN-13: 978-1957596037

First Printing June 2022
Published by 300 South Media Group

ACKNOWLEDGMENTS

I want to give much love and thanks to my teenager Atlas for helping me sort through all the poetry pieces that I have written over the years, narrowing it down to what you see here.

Great appreciation and thanks to my friend Cindy Walter and my fellow writer, Nicole Lyons for supporting me throughout the years, even when I faded into the unknown searching for myself.

Big hugs to my longtime friend Jay Long for believing in me, and putting this book together.

And a final thanks goes out to all the fans who have followed me for what seems like a lifetime on social media, always asking for a book, here's to you.

Lisa

TABLE OF CONTENTS

To the little girl I was,
who had to grow up too fast and too soon...

...we made it

Accustomed to Darkness

She had forgotten what innocence tasted like and often wondered if it tasted sweet, unlike the bitterness that life had left upon her tongue.

She had an old, worn-out soul wrapped up inside of her, and it sang of tales of love and horror.

It saddens me to know that such a creature of light is so accustomed to darkness, and it saddens me more to know, that she knows that too.

A Gentle Empath

She was never really alone, her loneliness kept her company, and on nights when the moon was full, they would exchange war stories like long-lost lovers. She had a way of making others feel alive when she was around them, especially those that were lost and broken. That made me sad, knowing that on occasion, she herself had forgotten what alive had felt like. A gentle empath with fierce eyes, eyes that held all the damage that was left behind by what life had done to her. I never knew a girl who played with darkness like her. I never knew a woman who called it home like she did; maybe it was because it loved her in a way that no one else would, or maybe it was because it wanted her for who she was. If she allowed you to get close to her, you could tell that she had to die a few times to have the dark rider bow at her feet, because even he knew better than to come for her alone.

An Odd One

She was an odd one;
an old soul living in a place not mentally evolved enough for her.
She never knew what to do with herself.
The wild within her was always wanting to be anywhere but here.
I think at times,
the only thing that calmed her soul was loving someone,
but that never turned out too well for her in the end.
Sometimes, she did find peace though, watching the moon high,
and telling it all her dirty little secrets.
I saw her one night sitting on her porch smiling,
and she looked at me and said,

"It was a good day today. The devil bowed at me,
and the angels watched in envy."

I Am Chaos

I was told
"Your name is chaos, and your heart is protected by demons."
I responded
"I am chaos and my heart is guarded by angels whose wings were
clipped by deceitful lovers."

✧ ◊★ · ★◊ ✧ ◊★ · ★◊ ✧

War With the Gods

She had a thing about loving people who were only
temporary. I came to believe she did that for a reason, and there
was a melody to the chaos that sang inside of her.

She was always at war with the gods, and restless from the hunger of
her demons. I wondered if anyone would ever see the dark beauty
that hid behind her fictitious smile, and if they would
be brave enough to stay and love her.

The Little Girl With the Big Eyes

She was the little girl with the big eyes and scraped knees, climbing
trees, and swinging on the tire swing in the backyard, head thrown back,
giggling as if her world was made of magic.
I often wondered where she got all that love from,
as a child loving broken toys,
to a woman loving people who would try and break her.
She never expected much from anyone, and I think
at times she could not wait to get back to whatever star she came from.
I think about her a lot, especially that day not too long ago.
It was one of those hot days when you thought you
would melt, and your chest felt too heavy to breathe.
She was there cutting roses in her yard, her favorite,
and I could see her closing her eyes smelling them,
as if it took her to another world.
So, I went up to her and she said to me,

"I am full of sleeping dragons, as I suppose most old
souls are, and this world cannot conquer me.
It has tried, but it has found that I bleed love and war."

Beautiful Soul

The angels have heard about you;
for I have whispered to them of a bound, beautiful soul.
They know of the chaos around you,
the anarchy within you,
and the freedom that you so desperately desire.

You are a beautiful soul
known amongst the stars,
as one who has been wished upon.
Remember that, when all
that you sometimes
see is darkness.

Battlefield of Life

I wish that I could tell you that everything will work out just as you have always dreamed of, but I won't.
You will crumble, you will splinter,
and you will feel the weight of the world.
There will be places in the dark that you will stay in,
no reservation required.
Sometimes, you will be your own destroyer, a taster of regret.
I wish that I could tell you that it will not be like this, but I won't.
What I will tell you is this, you are the beautiful one.
You are here with lungs filled with water,
brushing the ashes from your flesh, and you are not done yet.
This life has given you hell, and what do you do, smile, shake its hand and say, "Is that all you've got?"
The greatest battles ever fought are the ones that people never hear about, because most warriors choose to walk alone.
So, if you find yourself here on the battlefield of life, please know that you are not alone, and even the strongest need to be carried home sometimes.

The Reaper Wept

...and the reaper wept over mankind's cruelty,
for even he has more compassion for the ones he takes.

Kamikaze Kisses

Maybe, I do not know what love truly is,
except what I have read in all
that has been written.
I do know for sure, what love really isn't;
kamikaze kisses under the blood moon sky,
apocalyptic eyes on my bare skin thighs.

✧ ◊★ · ★◊ ✧ ◊★ · ★◊ ✧

Many Mates of the Soul

I was asked do you believe in soulmates, and I said,

"Yes, I believe there are many mates of the soul that pass in and out of
our lives. They see the rawness, the nakedness of what bleeds beneath
our skin. Most leave us behind, and we wonder why they came. Some
refuse to leave and we question why they stay. All who have come, leave
scars in their wake, and make us who we are."

Beautiful Black Soul

I can love, I have loved.
I am not insensitive, I feel.
I am Novocain,
numb to repetitious bullshit.

I'm not mean.
I've just become intolerant of meaningless words.
I am one of many beautiful black souls.

I will never satisfy the palate of the charlatans of this life.
I am too bitter,
distasteful to scathing eyes.

Barefoot in the Rain

She was afraid to unpack her heart anywhere
because every time she did, she was no longer wanted.
I could never understand the way of the world,
and how someone like her was always treated so poorly.
She knew of storms and of rainbows
and called the forsaken ones her friends.
I don't really remember her weeping too often,
       but at times,
I could hear the lone wolf in her whimper when she spoke.
She had sewn her sorrows in her clothing
and wore them like an evening dress.
I had asked her once why she liked to walk barefoot in the rain,
and she said

"It is the only time I feel like I belong somewhere,
like the tears of the earth and I are one."

Wild Beasts and Dark Wars

I wasn't scared of the dark, it had a way with me.
It found me at a young age, riding big wheels in the back yard,
climbing trees, and catching fireflies on warm summer nights.
The dark came dressed casually, smiling and giggling like a child. I
suppose it came how it needed to, to make me who I am.

Now hide away dark, tuck yourself between the memories of birthday
parties and sidewalk chalk drawings, hide away until the days I need
you. Let's grow up fast now, I have to, so I put away my crayons and my
little plastic toys, and I pet the wolves which now run free within me.

Everyone will know I am different, but they will never know why.
You see, they are laced together with sugary tales and pampered
bottoms, and me, well let's just say I am sewn together with wild beasts
and dark wars.

Phases of the Moon

I am all the phases of the moon,
but mostly I am the new moon;
for the dark is just as whole and beautiful as the light.
It is just hidden from those who still only see with their eyes.

✧ ◊★ · ★◊ ✧ ◊★ · ★◊ ✧

Empathic Soul

I am an empathic soul and stardust courses through my veins.
I must suffer, I must feel the cruelty of the world.
They cannot see that we are all connected,
they are merciless to each other.
I am love, I am not from here,
and I will not claim their ways as my own.

What a Warrior Looks Like

She hadn't quite been herself for some time, as if she knew who she was
back before the filthy hands of the world first touched her.
I never knew a soul could contain such darkness,
and not completely self-destruct.
I never knew a heart could hold so much sadness,
and still beat in tune.
I know what a warrior looks like—her—dark, fearful, and
full of a fire that won't die out no matter what you throw on it.

✧ ◇★ · ★◇ ✧ ◇★ · ★◇ ✧

Particular Way

It was a particular way the darkness wrapped itself around her as if it
was made to be worn only by her. She spoke to angels on the nights her
demons slept. I believe it was because she did not want them to hear
her weeping. I wish I knew why life had scolded her in the way that it
did, leaving marks too deep to heal, and I often wonder how it came to
be that she made pain her most beloved adversary.

All the Roads In Darkness

Come,
I know all the roads in darkness, and where they lead to.
I can take you home.

The Collector

She was a collector of unkept souls,
a keeper of unspoken dreams,
and she would skinny-dip in the moonlight on warm summer nights.
I watched her love the ones who would carve their name as pain into the
      belly of her soul,
and she would run her fingers over those scars
smiling, as if saying to herself,

"It will take more than that to break this beast."
Her pain made me weep, as the night weeps for
the stars, and I understood how wings were torn
from angels when they fell.

Carved My Pain

Did you find what you were searching for beneath the blanket of stars?
You hid behind the shadows when I tried to love you.
I carved my pain into the surface of the moon,
in hopes that you would see what you've done to me.

✧ ◊★ · ★◊ ✧ ◊★ · ★◊ ✧

A Dying Star

She felt used up,
spent,
a dying star in a still living universe.
Too many dark lands she had traveled within her soul,
to find her soul,
always returning with a smile
as if she just had the best time of her life.
What was darkness
but the girl who knew how to survive alone.

Chasing Rainbows

She was a girl chasing rainbows, a woman who knew about life the hard way, and you could tell she was not from around here.
She was not one to let people get too close to her.
I would watch her try, but she would always let go as if it hurt too much to hold on. She would rather be there for someone when their world is crumbling than let someone hold her while hers is falling apart.
She would not accept pity for her battles, no matter how bloodied she was. An earth-bound angel with a sword in each hand, taking on her nightmares and everyone else's too if she could.

I think back to a cool autumn day when the leaves were not quite ready to fall, but the wind would come taking them away.
It was then that I saw her alone, as she usually was, leaning against an old oak, one almost as old as her soul, and I wanted to know what the two of them were talking about, so I made my way to her,

      hearing her say,

"I am the first and last lone wolf born on a full moon night, wild, always running, searching for more like me, a descendant of the night, and I will make my darkness kneel to me."

Born a Warrior

It still feels like yesterday sometimes,
when you were there hiding in the shadows,
crying over the filth that had just washed away your innocence.

Little did you know that you were born a warrior
and warriors began just as you did;
momentarily stripped of their light,
filled with an eternal darkness,
and the very air that they would breathe would be exhaled as fire.

If I Was Myself

I thought that if I was myself,
and showed the world that I was love,
it would want me,
but I was wrong,
for it was the wolves who called me family.

✧ ◊★ · ★◊ ✧ ◊★ · ★◊ ✧

Loving Creatures

Most dark souls are empaths and tend to be the most loving of all creatures. They carry an endless well of compassion inside of them, and are soldiers of war, with their self-destructive nature.

A Rare One

She was a rare one, an empath living in a world that could never tame
her self-destructive nature.
As an old soul, she had a strange way about her.
She would turn other people's darkness into her own,
as if the darkness belonged only to her.

✧ ◊★ · ★◊ ✧ ◊★ · ★◊ ✧

I Know

I know what it means to love
I know how it feels to be discarded
I know what it means to hurt
I know how it feels to be nobody to somebody
I know of this as darkness
It knows of me as love

Arsenic Laced Heart

I am a danger to myself when it comes to love;
giving all that I have
until there is nothing left
but poetry written upon an arsenic-laced heart.

Chasing Butterflies

She was the little girl chasing butterflies in the wind and she dreamed only when the moon was full. Her soul was put together in a most peculiar way, hollow but full of the most beautiful darkness. What lies behind her eyes, I do not know, but I imagine it to be a field where she fought her most difficult battles. As far as I could tell, by what scars I could see, she was a goddess by her own right. She was the queen of pain, the guardian of misplaced souls and she felt like love was the edge of a rusty blade. I haven't seen her in quite some time, not since the catastrophe of her heart, but I will never forget the last thing she told me, "I was born out of the wreckage that left me and I became the love that shunned me."

Nobody Dreams

Nobody dreams of growing up to be an alcoholic,
an addict, a divorcee, broken, and depressed.
Bad things do happen to good people, and it is the
good people, the broken ones, that always seem to
have a vacancy in their hearts for those who do not
even give them a room in theirs.

✧ ◊★ · ★◊ ✧ ◊★ · ★◊ ✧

Battled Many Demons

I have battled many demons in my life.
Some left me quietly, many linger still.
They erupt a storm within me,
spawning tornadoes of chaos that I should try to put to rest,
but I am torn...
between becoming the storm or letting it pass.

Disappointed with the Stars

She was disappointed in the stars for losing all her wishes, but still left some on their doorstep, only when the moon was full.

I felt like she didn't really belong here, and was tired of the wantings of the world. They fed her God, and she choked on the sin of who she was, of who they made her believe she was.

If she had it to give, she would give until there was nothing left of herself, and her selflessness was her demise. I could hear her sometimes when her soul was weary, crying out,

"I am both the blade, and the wound. I am the devil in the night searching for my wings they took from me."

Diary of Heartache

She kept a diary of heartache on the top shelf of her soul,
and would write in it every day. I wanted to believe that she did not feel
like her only purpose in life was to be hurt by those she loved,
but she did.

Someone once told me she grew a garden of hope somewhere in the
shadows of her heart, and would go there often, pulling out the weeds
of disappointment.

I saw her the other day sitting alone on a bench
gazing up at the sky, and she looked at me and said,

"You know, I was born with all of this love inside of me, and the
uncontrollable desire to give it all away in hopes that someone would
love me too. The angels know not of the many wings I have burned in
the name of love, and I am so tired."

Shooting Star

I am the shooting star in the dark night,
clouded eyes fail to see my beauty.

Beauty not found on the surface,
but hidden deep within my core.

I illuminate the sky with only shards of my tormented heart,
in hopes that someone will wish upon me.

✧ ◊★ · ★◊ ✧ ◊★ · ★◊ ✧

Newfound Darkness

I am not pretty like them
I am beautiful like me
I do not need anyone to fight my battles for me
I earned every scar I bear
And I will still love me in my newfound darkness

Hallways In Her Eyes

She has hallways in her eyes
leading to rooms that are filled with war-worn stories,
and when the light hits in just the right way,
you can see the phoenix in her grinning,
as if saying, "bring it".

✧ ◇★ · ★◇ ✧ ◇★ · ★◇ ✧

Good Intentions

I have not always lived in the best ways, but I have always had good intentions. I love with all I have, even when I have nothing. I give and I have given to those who leave me on a throne of madness....but still, I rise.

Dirty Secrets

I had forgotten how your words were like dirty secrets,
and how they rained down battles upon my flesh.

A Moment of Sympathy

"I am sorry that I never believed in you, that I hurt you and made you feel alone. Forgive me for all the cruel things that I said about you when you were already feeling down. I am sorry that I didn't love you, and that I even hated you at times. Please forgive me for keeping you in darkness when I knew you were worthy of light."

Things I have said to myself in a moment of sympathy.

✧ ◇★ · ★◇ ✧ ◇★ · ★◇ ✧

Three Words

I have heard that three words,
and three words alone can save me;
that I cannot move on until I hear them,
until I say them and mean them.
So, here I go
"I forgive me."

Confession

I must confess to myself who I really am.
I am an unrestrained lover, dark and amorous.
I walk a line that has cataclysmic results.
I love myself, I hate myself.
I have an endangered soul and a corrupted mind.
My heart is in critical condition, on the verge of
never being revived again.
Yet, I will love and love freely.
I am my own punisher.
I want to be good, but I enjoy being bad.
I am alive, although I feel dead at times.
I am not like most, yet I am like some.
Crazy, with a dash of humility.
So I will no longer chain myself to who I am not,
and with that I can be free.

My Place In The Sky

She was the girl with the unruly heart, the woman with the unsettling soul, and she dreamed in pale shades of blue.
There was a sort of melancholy to her stride, as if the world had beat down on her a little too hard.
She knew death by name, and death would never forget hers,
as the one that got away.
I believe she had a darkness to her, the kind that you can never get rid of. She had a light to her too, the kind that you will never forget.
She mostly kept her feelings to herself, only allowing a few to get to know her, and if you were lucky enough to be one of them, she would leave behind an aroma of love and hope in your soul.
I think the stars left her here, and she yearned to get back to them, back to where she belonged.
I remember one night in particular, it was a full moon, God how she loved the moon, and the way it understood her.
She looked up at the moon, took a deep breath, and said to me,

"I am the victor, the victim, the soulful, the soulless, the lover, the despiser, and I have earned my place in the sky."

Executioner

She used to say that she wanted someone to love her, not for her looks or what she had to give, but for her many scars and empty pockets. I think she felt like love was half-written promises and broken notes that were only found in songs written by fairytale poets.

She was strong when it came to anything but love, and I had watched her rise over and over again from the graves that life had buried her in. It was just the other day that I saw her sitting out by a lonesome willow tree, and I thought that maybe I should go sit with her.

I went to her and sat down, not saying a word. She was looking down at the ground twisting the grass between her fingers, and I could see her smiling when she said,

"I am shattered glass and twisted metal, a lover of forbidden fruit and cast away souls. They bring me pain, and I give them love. This is my life, this is who I am; the executioner of my own heart. I will never be broken, only chipped in places that I will only ever see."

Innocent Smile

She was the little girl with the innocent smile, and she painted her life in off shades of grey. An old soul with old battle wounds, who held the hands of those who were outsiders and vagabonds. She was a woman with an uncanny smile, a soldier, a lover, and a keeper of secrets and foolish dreams. Death couldn't have her, life couldn't bind her, and the dark was the only one who could understand her pain.

✧ ◇★ · ★◇ ✧ ◇★ · ★◇ ✧

Daughter of Light

She was the daughter of light, the mother of darkness, and she laughed at pain, as if she was its nemesis. An angel, lonely but fierce, one who burned her wings for those she cared for. She was a silent soldier, whose tears turned to steel. A woman, who gathered her broken pieces, and built a throne out of them. A throne she earned, and she sat upon it gracefully, battle-scarred and proud. She would not let go of herself, not ever again, not for anyone or anything.

What Makes a Man

What makes a man a man, is it what he has to offer the world in material, or is it what the world has forged him into through many lashings?

Some are full in pocket, and others are full in soul.
Some pay their dues ten-fold, and some never pay at all.

A man that has had to breathe darkness as air will possess one of the most beautiful souls of all.

Greatest Love Story

To listen to someone's broken heart and tired soul without judgment can sometimes be the greatest love story they will ever know.

A Fistful of Heaven

She grew up in a small town, loved old houses, old books, and the boys who would never love her back.

She liked to take roads unfamiliar to her, wondering where they went, hoping it would lead her back to where she came from.

I can tell you that she knew she didn't belong anywhere or to anyone that would ever claim her, and you could see it in her eyes, those damn eyes of hers.

They swam with things most people feared, and you could see the bite marks that they left on her soul.

She had a way with people, or maybe I should say they had their way with her, and she stopped expecting anyone to stay anymore,

at least not after they got what they wanted.

I suppose that is why she was just as good at letting go as she was at loving.

I miss talking to her, she always spoke of otherworldly things, things that made you still believe in dragons, made you believe in love.

The last time we spoke was under a blood red sky, and she smiled in a way that I will always remember, when she said,

"I could give up, but I don't. I've got a fistful of heaven, and way too much hell left to give."

Written Into the Night Sky

...and I suppose there must be those who have found their knights and fair maidens, their kings and queens; for their stories are written in poems, and found in the stars.

Then there are those of us who have only found dark horseman and sinister damsels, jesters and wenches.

So, we read and we hope, and we dream of becoming
the poem written into the night sky.

Haunted Alleys

She was not sure where she was going, but she was definitely sure where she had been; haunted alleys in her soul, placing flowers on the graves of her past selves.

The years had been too long and too heavy for her, and her heart overflowed with unrequited love.

A sensitive soul in an insensitive world, giving until there is nothing left to hold onto; no rope left behind for her, as she jumped from cliffs to save those she loved.

She crumbled in the night, and battled in the day, only to find herself singing lullabies to her demons.

No one knew her as well as the moon did, and it wept for her, refusing to let her go into the night alone.

Who stayed, when everyone else fled in her time of battle? It was the silence that never left her side——the silence left behind by those she cared for.

I never knew a woman who wore heartache as beautifully as she did, and at times, I wondered who needed to.

A Bit Odd

I suppose I am a bit odd,
not finding comfort in materialistic things.
I prefer starry skies, burning candles,
and the souls that most people shun.
Some would say that I am a freak,
and I would say that I am proud to be called one.

✧ ◊★ · ★◊ ✧ ◊★ · ★◊ ✧

I Walk Alone

I don't belong to the blue skies and sunny days. My place is beneath the stars, in the dead of night. I am a freak, a loner, wandering amongst the things most people shun, judged by strangers and family just alike. I don't ask for their acceptance to be who I am. I walk alone with my demons, and together we ask for no one's approval.

Head in the Clouds

There were those that would say she kept her head in the clouds, and I guess in a way they were right. She was home up there I suppose, closer to the moon, closer to her confidant, the protector of her darkest secrets. Her soul, in all its vastness, was a lush forest of love and pain, a place where angels went to cry. You could hear faint laughter in the distance as if she was mocking her demons, and all their attempts to destroy her.

She commanded the dark, summoned the light, and somewhere in between she would find rest. As a lover of broken souls, she was a companion to their suffering and seemed to welcome it with such fervor. At times, she grew weary of life and all its demands; so much so, that she would forget to put pieces of herself back together as if she could just do without them.

Warrior's Blood

She felt like love wasn't meant for someone like her,
maybe she was only made to love and not be loved.
At least, that is what she believed.
I could see it in her, the loneliness,
and how it wrapped itself around her smile.
She couldn't help how she felt, a stranger in her own skin,
a soul out of place, wishing someone would call her home.
There were beautiful gardens growing inside of her,
and there were graveyards too,
filled with everyone who said they loved her and lied.
I often wondered how she could go on,
but then I remembered what she told me on a cold winter night,

"Many have tried and failed in breaking my spirit but I know what a
warrior's blood tastes like, for it flows through my veins."

Hold My Halo

Most times I will tell you
"I am the calm before the storm"
but sometimes I will say
"Here, hold my halo I'm going in"

Big Talker

He wasn't a big talker, especially when it came to his past and one could only imagine how that fire started in his eyes.

Some would say he was cold-hearted just by the way he looked. He wasn't though, he just gave too much of his soul to those he's cared for, and it left him a bit empty.

He didn't smile often, but when he did, you could tell that he was a man that had been force-fed darkness.

Too Much of Myself

I suppose I demanded too much of myself. I knew that what I had become could no longer tolerate who I was. There was a battle brewing between them, and I could not choose a side to standby. I believe there was a part of me that enjoyed my darkness. It was a jealous lover, and I thrive on that.

✧ ◇★ · ★◇ ✧ ◇★ · ★◇ ✧

Dark Days and Darker Nights

I may not be the person that I dreamed of becoming,
but damn,
I sure have survived some dark days, and even darker nights;
and that has to count for something.

Fireflies and Honey

Her soul was made of fireflies and honey, anarchy and angels. She had a heart full of revolutions and white flags, secrets, and sacrifices. She was the silly girl who collected lost moments, and empty places. remember her with her head in the clouds daydreaming of love while drawing hearts on blank sheets of paper. She was the girl who grew up too fast and learned about pain too soon. I believe she felt that life did not like her so much, but the way she made people shine you would have never guessed that. It was a miserably hot day, the hottest I can remember since I was a child. I saw her sitting poolside drinking what looked like something sweet but toxic, kind of like her. She waved at me and smiled in a way that gave me both shivers and butterflies. I thought twice before walking over to her because she could always see into my soul; and before I could say a word she said,

"Be careful who you cry out to in the middle of the night, it is not just God who is listening."

Pocket Full of Fury

You believe the catastrophe of the universe began in you, and that even darkness knows better than to speak your name. Hard times know you all too well as a fighter, and there have been moments when it damn near beat the life out of you, but you never gave in.

You've got a pocket full of fury, a bag full of blades, and you were just getting started.

✧ ◊★ · ★◊ ✧ ◊★ · ★◊ ✧

Certain Kind of Madness

There was a certain kind of madness to how I loved.
My passion came at a high price.
At times,
I would have given my soul in order to receive the love I had to offer.
It always left me covered in darkness.

Sensitive Soul

Having a sensitive soul means becoming numb on the inside
while breathing life into others.
It means being misunderstood, mistreated, and even hated at times.
It is leaving no love for yourself
because you gave it all away to those undeserving.
It means waiting in the darkness
for those who would not even do the same.

Having a sensitive soul is not a weakness as some may think,
        but a strength.
Sensitive souls are born warriors,
capable of enduring great suffering and heartache,
and without them, the world would crumble.

I Will Bring You Back

Tell me where you think you lost yourself.
I will go find you, and bring you back.

✧ ◊★ · ★◊ ✧ ◊★ · ★◊ ✧

Long Forgotten

If you happen to stumble upon me in the darkest corners of life,
and by chance fall in love with my heart,
I will offer to you, the pieces of my soul that were neglected by others.
Not to put them back together, but to align them with the pieces of
yours that have been long forgotten.

Hunting Werewolves

The other kids were playing with their toys
while I was out hunting werewolves in the forest.

Her Rising

She didn't ask for the past to be as it was.
She would have chosen differently.
Whether fate or circumstance, it became a part of her.
A universe of anguish, a galaxy of love, intertwined into what she had
become—part midnight, part sunlight.
I couldn't tell if she was alive, she felt like it.
Death would have said hello, at least I hope so.
Many had stood by and witnessed her suffering.
Yet, few knew of her rising.
It was beautiful: steel wings, bruised fists, and the demons of her
persecutors bowed in tears.

Angry With the World

He was angry with the world, like most of us.

He had lost family and friends, broke past lovers, and they broke him.

Work, well let's just say it was a temporary distraction, an escape from thinking about thinking.

He never shed a tear, at least not one that anyone could see.

Inside of him though, was a torrential storm.

He held onto memories of who he was like a life preserver,

to keep himself from drowning.

✧ ◇★ · ★◇ ✧ ◇★ · ★◇ ✧

Life Had Been Tough on Him

Life had been tough on him,

and he often drifted to the edge.

He loved his drink and his bud.

They made him feel like life was a bit kinder to him,

and I suppose I could not blame him for that.

Fire-Breathing Bohemian

When the world tries to break you,
run back into the wild,
 and remember who you are.
You're a fire-breathing bohemian,
with galaxies dripping from your lips,
and no man nor woman
can fuck with you.

✦ ◇★ · ★◇ ✦ ◇★ · ★◇ ✦

Sunday Morning Stroll

Satan wept at the sound of her name,
for her soul was where dragons went to die,
and to her, hell was just another Sunday morning stroll.

Heretic

I am a heretic,
defiant of the boundaries set before me.
I am a beast, hungry for erotic love,
thirsty for liquid light to illuminate the dark within me.
I do not belong in the pack of society.
I am rogue, wild, an outcast,
and I shall bare my teeth to those who look down upon me.
For, I cannot ignore the howls of who I am,
and I will not bow down to what others think I should be.

◇ ◊★ · ★◊ ◇ ◊★ · ★◊ ◇

Listen

Listen to the words I cannot say
Feel the emotions I do not express
Leave your opinions at the doorstep of my heart
For I am unhinged, an outcast,
and I need you to know
that I am haunted by things that you could never fathom
So, for a moment, keep silent, and hear me weep
Be witness to what it is like to be damned

Born Old

I always wondered where she was always rushing off to; the next stoplight, the next stop sign, her next death. She was born old, not in the way of man, but old in the way of the universe.

I do not believe that she has ever really felt young as a child or as a woman. I guess most old souls never do. She was out of place here among the land dwellers, and at times she was out of her mind. I can only imagine the arguments that she had in her head with her demons. I believe that is where she fought her most devastating battles, in her mind, and you could see the twisted wreckage in her eyes. I believe that love began and ended within her, in such a selfless, destructive way and she had a way with the outcasts, and I suppose fallen angels always do.

Quiet Your Screams

Quiet your screams, my love.
The wolves are done feasting on the remains of your heart.
Go now,
and know that there is nothing left behind to harm you.

✧ ◊★ · ★◊ ✧ ◊★ · ★◊ ✧

Calloused Heart

Baby, I know that your heart is calloused, and at times you feel as if you are not worthy of happiness.

That is not true, you have just given too much of your soul to cheap love and fake people.

Keep Your Knife

Keep your knife, my love.
For, I have many that I have pulled out of my back,
and hung them as trophies on the walls of my soul.

The Way of the World

I am not beautiful
In the way of the world

I am scarred
With ten thousand lashings

I am beautiful
Not in the way of the world

I am love
With twenty thousand lashings

I am not
The way of the world

I am
My own world

I Cannot Claim

I cannot claim too many things in my life,
but I can claim these things:
I have been death's adversary, life's mystery,
and love's hardest shell to crack.
I cannot claim to any fame or fortune
except that which has left me famous in hell
and rich in the knowledge of survival.

✧ ◊★ · ★◊ ✧ ◊★ · ★◊ ✧

Pieces

I broke off pieces of my heart,
and called it love,
serving it to those who renamed it pain.
I chipped away pieces of my soul,
and called it home,
welcoming those who renamed it hell.

Walk With Me

Come, walk with me for a while. I want to tell you about the times that I felt like dying, when the world was not my friend, life was not my lover, and death spoke to me only in tongues. Don't speak, just listen, and it doesn't even matter if you understand. I made it through the flames of heartache, and I want you to know that it was worth burning just to see myself smile again.

✧ ◇★ · ★◇ ✧ ◇★ · ★◇ ✧

Come Walk With Me

"Come, walk with me for a while." said the moon,
"Let us go back to when we first met,
back to when you looked at me like I was magic and the wolf in you called me its only lover."

Disconnected

I am disconnected with myself and the world.
A hollowed-out soul, not by choice, at least I don't think so.

There are those who get destroyed by life.
There are those who destroy themselves in the search of feeling alive.

Then there are those who are like me,
both the prey and the predator of life.
We are the ones who have led our hearts into darkness for love more
times than we can count, and have lit our souls on fire for others more
times than that.

Reruns

I cannot turn back time,
and change the things that I wish had never happened.

I can try and keep what is left of my life though,
gather up the pieces, and create a mosaic of beautiful madness.

I suppose it is all an old soul can do, I suppose that is all any of us can do
sometimes; wait for the good memories to overtake the bad,
until we anticipate them like reruns of our favorite TV show.

Wild Beasts Call Home

She learned about heaven as a child, and how hell was for
naughty little girls. I suppose in her eyes heaven wasn't a
place she would ever see, and hell, well hell's door was
always open.
I have never seen anyone love like her, her body was a
temple of madness, and her heart was an alter for
destruction. Why anyone would ever let her go or hurt her
was beyond me, but they all did.
It wasn't just her love that was endless, it was her
selflessness. She would suffer for anyone if she could,
forgetting about her broken bones to fix theirs.
I had always thought she was made for someplace else,
someplace where others like her could run free, and get
the love they deserved.
She was not someone you could forget easily, once she
touched your soul with hers, you would never be the same.
The last time I saw her she said to me,

"My mother didn't tell me about the dark, I don't know if it
was because she didn't believe in it or because she didn't
think it would find me. I am not a bad person, just untamed you see, I
mean my soul is, it is where the wild beasts call home."

Moonshine and Midnight

She was moonshine and midnight, angelic grin and soft sin.
She sang in wolf's tune.
She was born a full moon.

Relentless Heart

There is no greater truth than a soul that is born with a relentless heart will survive in a broken world—they always do.

✧ ◊★ · ★◊ ✧ ◊★ · ★◊ ✧

Running Into Yourself

Sometimes, when you are running away from yourself you will run into yourself, and when you do, you will see how beautiful the demolition of who you were looks in your eyes.

Hold My Head High

I cannot say that I know everything about life, but I can say this:
There had been times when life had kicked my ass and times
when I had kicked its ass.

There had been moments when I would have chosen death
over going on, and there had been moments when death
chose me.

At times, I had been my own destructor, and all I knew was darkness.
My body was a battleground, and I had more scars than I could count.
I had a closet full of regrets, and a heart full of blades.

It all seemed so futile. A sick cycle that would never end, and I
knew that there was only one thing that I could do. So, I beat down who
I was with bloodied fists, and began feeling proud of who I was
becoming.

I was a badass for making it this far, and for that,
I could hold my head high.

A Field of Fire

I buried my pain beneath a smile that wasn't mine,
and I wanted to break.
Yes, I wanted to laugh in the eyes of those who attempted to destroy me,
but instead, I fought off my own self-destruction.

Who could destroy me, but me?

I would not give them the pleasure of killing my self-love,
and I would not go down without a fight.
I never imagined as a child having to fight my way through life,
and I never dreamed I would become a survivor of untold horrors.

If you find me in a field of fire, take me home,
brush me off, and say "you made it."

Stay With Me

"Stay with me a little longer," she said to the moon.
"I have so much more I want to tell you."

The Never Girl

I am the never girl
The half-past midnight
I am the always girl
The rider on the edge
I am the before and after, do it again girl
The coffee and the pain
I am the dark corner girl
The keeper of secrets
I am the love girl
The scars of war
I am the good enough for me girl
The last chapter read

Let's Dance

When all that remains of yourself cries out
"No more!"
Don't wait for the world to understand,
drag your demons out and say,
"Come on, let's dance."

✧ ◊★ · ★◊ ✧ ◊★ · ★◊ ✧

Thorns and Stormy Nights

She loves thorns and stormy nights but was told to love flowers and sunny days.
I watched her live in free verse and fall in silent sonnets.
She often thought of leaving this world but held on to the day that someone would understand the lyrics of her soul.
I thought about her as she sat beneath the weeping willow saying.

"I remember the day the reaper came for me, and I told him I had learned to dance in the nightmare that was created, and he would have to ask for the next dance."

Black Sheep

Black sheep pay no attention to the insults of the mind-conditioned herds. They follow their own set of rules, running side by side with their family. Those who will always have their back. Those who have been labeled as wolves.

✧ ◊★ · ★◊ ✧ ◊★ · ★◊ ✧

I Have Run

I have run with the wolves,
slept with the lions,
deserted the pack, and fled the pride.
I am a loner among lovers,
finding solace in my lone wolf cry.

My Demons

My demons are my own.
Who are you to judge how I deal with what belongs to me.

Outcast Soul

I do not fit in anywhere
Or belong to anyone
But, if I come across an outcast soul
An odd one such as myself
One covered in silken dreams
Drenched in satin nightmares
A scar bearer
One who has found themselves
In darkness
Then I will stay with them
For a little while anyhow
Gazing at the stars
Trying to find our way back home

Heart of a Dragon

She has a heart of a dragon,
and eyes like the moon,
She's a mermaid at sunrise,
and a wolf by noon.
The universe is her lover,
and chaos her tune.

✧ ◇★ · ★◇ ✧ ◇★ · ★◇ ✧

Simple Person

I suppose I am a simple person,
finding joy in the little things;
like staying up late telling stories,
fireflies burning in the night,
the stars winking at the moon,
and the words' I Love You' when they are true.

Felt a Bit Dusty

I felt a bit dusty, run-over, and I became weary of escaping the escapism. My smile was worn-out, and it looked more like a facade, and I hoped that it would soon turn to stardust.

I knew I was born a fighter, my scars proved that, and I knew that I was strong, my life reflected that.

Death knew not what a difficult nemesis I would be, and I did not take into account the consequences of holding onto life.

I was older, yes, wiser, not so sure, more like seasoned to a life of turmoil. Complaining, a language I refuse to use, and so, I suffer in silence, reign in survival, and sit on a throne of hope.

Scattered Into the Wind

I grew exhausted of the ramblings of the shallow-hearted.

So, my mind sat weary and lonely in a corner of hell,

like a child being punished.

I wanted to know what heaven felt like,

and if there was any truth to love.

The vanity and selfishness of this world could kiss my ass.

I could show them what selflessness looked like.

It was burning your own heart at times,

and watching the ashes scattered into the wind.

The Rains Came

The rains came and went,
just as you did,
and I wondered if you ever found the love that I gave you.
It was right where you left it,
strewn amongst the ruins of my soul.

✧ ◇★ · ★◇ ✧ ◇★ · ★◇ ✧

Tired of Feeling

I think I am tired, tired of feeling.
I want to leave these stones in my lungs,
and sharpen the razors on my tongue.
I want to hide in the black sunsets,
where their lies can never hurt me.

In a Field

I want to lie in a field beneath the light of the moon,
a place unknown to the stars.

Someplace where my troubles might not find me,
even if it is just until the wind weeps no more.

I want to look at the midnight sky instead of gazing upon the darkness
inside of me, although, both are devastatingly beautiful.

✧ ◊★ · ★◊ ✧ ◊★ · ★◊ ✧

An Offering

I am an offering of shattered glass dreams,
and in the black forest of my soul lies the child,
the one who left me behind to seek comfort in the melody of the
weeping woods.

Darkness On Fire

Your final soulmate will never leave you in the dark that has found you.
They will set their own darkness on fire to light your home.

Gaze Upon The Moon

I gaze upon the moon
and it smiles at me,
watching over me
as a lover should,
not turning away
when I need it the most.

Yet, as past lovers,
I suppose it only shone when it was in his favor,
leaving me to nights of darkness,
wondering when love would appear again,
hoping maybe,
for once, it would stay.

Coattails of Storms

I am only human,
and I think that maybe they forget that.
They want perfect,
but I am a catastrophe,
always clinging to the coattails of storms.

✧ ◊★ · ★◊ ✧ ◊★ · ★◊ ✧

Sail Into Storms

I suppose I have never been one to sail away from storms.
Instead, I have always headed straight into them.
Maybe, it was because I needed the wreckage to feel alive,
or maybe
it was the only way to see the beauty in my ruins after I had survived.

I Love Lost Souls

I love lost souls, those as lost as mine,
and in an odd way, I adore this darkness
that has become my most devoted lover.

I have closed my mind to a thousand dreams,
 to ten thousand lies, and hid my eyes from a million sorrows.

There are moments when my depression depresses me,
and I yearn to be in a field of blooming poppies
with those who are like me.

At times,
I find it hard to move forward when everyone still lives in my past,
and I often wonder why they only remember me as a defiant
when I was love too.

Hid In the Eye of the Storm

I hid in the eye of the storm and wondered
if life might have broken me.
I thought to myself, that to be broken meant that
maybe I could be fixed, and that at one time
I must have been whole.
My life had been undeniably damaged by the
world, there was no fixing that, and my soul
had become a wanderer, forever searching
for that nameless peace.

These thoughts comforted me.

It meant that I was not broken.
I was only incomplete.

Comfortable

She was most comfortable in her skin when she was with the things that allowed her to be herself. Like the moon and the sea and the cracked mirror that hung in her room for only her to see.

✧ ◊★ · ★◊ ✧ ◊★ · ★◊ ✧

Too Real

You don't have to love me.
Hell, I don't even care if you like me,
because I'm my own kind of fucked up.
A little too real for this fake-ass world

Within My Silence

Within my silence,
I miss you.
Hidden in the chambers of my mind,
I shall find you.
Echoes of your voice still surround me,
traces of your touch still binds me.
Locked away in me,
I will keep you,
not holding on,
yet, not letting go,
only allowing you to sleep within me,
kept in a place that I know you will always be.

Angels With Tucked Wings

I have heard many tales of angels, but my favorite one is about those
that have tucked their wings away.
Those with closed minds and hearts cannot recognize them, because
they are people like you and I.
The fallen, the scarred, and yet still so full of strength and love.
They are the givers, the unconditional lovers,
and this world will never be their home.
They are the outsiders, the freaks, the loners,
the ones who get overlooked.
They are the trampled, the abused, the lost, and the lonely; and if you
are so fortunate to befriend one of these angels,
I suggest you never let them go.

The Spook

...and then there is me;
the oddball, the 'spook', the mystique.
The one that nobody takes the time to get to know.
I am more than the moon is to the night,
and I wonder if there is anyone who cares to know that.

✧ ◊★ · ★◊ ✧ ◊★ · ★◊ ✧

I am a Lover

I am a lover of odd things,
a friend to the abandoned, unwanted,
and outcast souls whom society has deemed unlovable,
because I too have felt this.

Lost Inside

I just smoked my last cigarette, and as I exhaled into the brisk winter air, I thought to myself 'what the hell am I doing with my life'?

Somewhere, along the way, I inhaled someone else's dreams, and exhaled my own.

Now, I am lost inside the labyrinth of my mind, needing constant sedation for my thoughts, demanding tranquility for my emotions.

I am frightened of myself, and that is a damn shame.

One Thing

I am not good at a lot of things,
especially life, love, and containing who I am.
I am good at one thing though,
and that is survival.

✧ ◇★ · ★◇ ✧ ◇★ · ★◇ ✧

That Girl

That girl knows about love,
knows about pain,
and sometimes
she mistakes one
for the other.

The Let Go Girl

She was the let go girl, the hold on too long girl, the lover
of simple things and forgotten people.

I remember her as a child, playing in the freshly raked pile of leaves in
her front yard, catching lightning bugs at dusk, and riding her bike as if
all the world could see how fast she could go.

I remember her back before life showed her its ugliness, back before her
tear-soaked pillows, and at times I think she remembered too.

She was an old soul with broken bones and scars, and I believe the word
pain originated from her.

There were stories in her, beautiful and sad stories, and sometimes she
would read them to me.

She would crumble herself into pieces for those she loved, even if they
did not love her back, and I think she had angels weeping in her soul.
It has been a long time since I have seen her, and I will never forget the
last thing she said to me

"I became the sword that failed to slay me. I have seen darkness, it has
seen me, and it is the one that will tremble at the sound of my name."

Back Together

She doesn't need anyone to keep her from coming undone.
What she wants is someone to hold the pieces
while she tries to put herself back together.

✦ ◇★ · ★◇ ✦ ◇★ · ★◇ ✦

I Am Like Me

I am not like them
I am like me
I am not someone who wants to be saved
I am an old soul, a soldier of war
and I was made to carry more pain than others

Her Pain

The light couldn't have her
The dark couldn't hold her
And the moon was the only one who could swallow her pain

Life's Attempt To Smite Me

I know that at times you feel that the sun rises without a heart, and sets without a soul. I know that you are weary of the mumbling about love, and the ramblings about life.

Love has come, gone, or has never stepped foot at your door. You feel as if life has got it out for you, and you cannot figure out what the fuck you did to deserve it. Yes, you hold yourself accountable for some of the roads that you chose to travel, but you followed your heart, isn't that what they told you to do?

I cannot tell you that everything will shine as bright as you want it to, or taste as sweet as you would like it to, or if love will ever brush by you, but I can tell you how I live where you are.

I have become my own soulmate, resting my heart within my hands. I laugh at life, and its attempts to smite me. I am my own best friend because I will never leave my side. If life does not grant me serenity and a lover, I know that I am armored well, and nothing will ever break me.

I Felt Alive

The music was loud, and I felt alive.
I felt good about the things that haunted me,
but I wanted it,
I needed it to be louder,
so that it would swallow the horrors within me.

✦ ◊★ · ★◊ ✦ ◊★ · ★◊ ✦

Hummed of Heartache

She hummed of heartache
like most people sang of love,
with grace and admiration,
and an appreciation to be brushed by such things

In the Arms of Hope

Courageous are the ones
who die violently in the arms of hope,
only to rise again stronger
than they were before

✧ ◊★ · ★◊ ✧ ◊★ · ★◊ ✧

Three Things

If my life has taught you anything
I hope it is these three things:
Hell is real
So is love
And both can be survived

Life, the Radio Station

Life, the radio station that always plays your favorite song or plays nothing but shit, I guess it's just like that sometimes. Crying, I do it, not always out loud, don't really care who knows it or not. I kind of figure if my soul is too full of raging waters, better to cry than to kick some ass. Some may beg to differ, can't quite blame them for that, this world is filled with some awful creatures, and might as well kickstart some karma if you can. Love, hmmm, should I even go there? Some people know about it, others sell and buy it at yard sales, cheap effective, and disposable. Then there are those who are love, they are the ones who keep this world from burning to ashes, and if you come across one of them you can bet that they have more scars than you have stories. Heaven and hell, demons and angels, God, Gods, and believers of universal things; I don't really care what you believe in or not. I've seen believers turn their backs on me, and nonbelievers take off their shoes and walk on hot coals with me, seen the reverse too. In the big picture of life, by that you're a good person or not, there will always be evil waiting to greet us with a bouquet of flowers.

Sensual Traveler

I do not want to believe that I have been designed to be alone. My soul has been split too many times, and I have become my own dark lover. I care for everybody and nobody, loving with everything or nothing. I am the outsider, the loner, and the sensual travel of the free-spirited world.

There must be others out there like me.

◆ ◇★ · ★◇ ◆ ◇★ · ★◇ ◆

She Had a Deep Soul

She had a deep soul and a darkness that was even deeper. I would often find her drifting away from the world, maybe trying to find her way back home, or quite possibly just searching for others like her. She was always trying to turn people's nightmares into rainbows and had forgotten what it was like to not live in one. I think if there is such a thing as a devil, then he most likely learned how to dance from her.

Midnight Storms and Raging Waters

She didn't have a lot of friends. She preferred it that way, because the world had betrayed her too many times.

The little girl inside of her had fallen asleep long ago, but still dreamed of unicorns running free.

She said that dragons had left flames burning inside of her, and didn't know where she belonged.

I will never forget her eyes, God her eyes spoke with the most beautiful madness when she said,

"I have nothing left in me but midnight storms and raging waters."

Sleeping Beast

Life did its best to break you now didn't it?
But all it did was awaken a beast that it should have left sleeping.

Breathe In Hope and Exhale Chaos

You have made a lot of mistakes in your life, and probably will make many more. Your intentions are good, but your heart always manages to make a mess of things. Most people would not understand what it is like to dig yourself out of a grave, only to find yourself buried in another one. You sometimes feel like the universe says "I am going to fuck you up, but just enough so that you are left still breathing." There are times you want to let go, and times you want to hold on to see if all of this pain will be worth it. You were a child once, a dreamer, looking up at the clouds in awe, imagining yourself flying through the air. That child is still in you saying, "It's okay, you can still dream, let me show you how."

So, when you feel like you are at the end of it all, listen to the child in you saying, "breathe in hope, and exhale chaos."

Tea Parties

The other kids were outside running around pretending to kill monsters, while I was inside having tea parties with them.

✧ ◊★ · ★◊ ✧ ◊★ · ★◊ ✧

Eyes as Big as Her Heart

She was the little girl with eyes as big as her heart, and dreams
as grand as her soul.
She was the dark princess playing with dragons, teaching them how to
breathe flames.
To her, the outcasts made the best friends, because they were
the only ones who understood what it is like to be born with a self-
destructive soul.

Renditions of Myself

I have slayed many renditions of myself in my life:
the savage beast,
the gentle lover,
the trampled giver.
I've lost my will,
gained my soul,
became a dreamer,
a realist,
a rebel,
a follower,
and a collector of love and pain.

I collaborate with my demons,
and seek clarity from my angels.

My past is filth and beauty.
My present is dark and enlightening,
and my future...well, who the fuck knows?

Brave Ones

Brave are the ones
who stand on the edge
of sanity and do not flinch.

✧ ◊★ · ★◊ ✧ ◊★ · ★◊ ✧

I Am Love

...and if the world asks about me,
tell them that I do have a soul.
Tell them that I am love,
and that I am not what I have done in the past.

A Few Fights

You could tell that she had been in a few fights with life and that hell had engraved its name on her bones. I think she was part midnight, and when the moon hung low, she would howl out to it in one long, somber cry. Her soul was a battlefield, a graveyard of untold stories of survival, and I had watched her carve her name into many tombstones.

I believe the phoenix got their wings from her, and she willingly gave them, reducing herself to ashes for those she loved.

Which star brought her here, I do not know, but I hope one day she will find her way back.

✧ ◇★ · ★◇ ✧ ◇★ · ★◇ ✧

Something Sexy

There was something sexy about the way she picked the bones of her enemies from her teeth.

Unfinished Novel

I am an unfinished novel.

Each chapter is filled with all the characters from my life.

Love, happiness, pain, and sorrow is the ink that I write with.

The good chapters are too short, and I wish they would last longer.

The painful chapters are too long,

and I beg for the next chapter to begin.

At times, I want to skip to the end, to see if it was all worth it.

Yet, I turn my pages with patience, in hopes, that the next chapter will

be filled with all the things that have only existed in my dreams.

Some Girls

Some girls are born to live like queens in fairytales,
and some girls like her,
are born to fight the monsters that live in them.

Soulmate of Storms

I've never been anyone's cat's meow.
I'm more like a lone wolf's howl.
I have no tales of fairies and queens,
only grayed-out alleys with dark dreams.
I care not of society's norms.
I am a freak, an outcast, a soulmate of storms.

✧ ◇★ · ★◇ ✧ ◇★ · ★◇ ✧

Never Knew Gentle

She never knew gentle
She only knew fierce
Love made her
Pain molded her
and the night called her its own

Never Forgotten

You were ripped away from me
And I feel as if a part of me
Has been ripped away too
So, I will carry in me
Your hopes and dreams
I will carry with me
Your smile and laughter
Inside my soul
I will keep my love for you
Inside my soul
I will always remember
Your love for me
I will patiently await the moment
When we will meet again
In the next life
So, until then,
I will learn to live
Without you
Never forgotten
Always loved

My Prey Is Love

I belong to no pack,
no pack belongs to me.
My prey is love, I hunger for it,
and alone I hunt it.
Yet, every scent I have followed has only led me into darkness,
and in darkness, I have survived.

✦ ◊★ · ★◊ ✦ ◊★ · ★◊ ✦

In the Shower

She would be in the shower scrubbing her skin, as if she was scrubbing
her soul clean of all the filth that life had left on her.

Rainy-day Eyes

She was the girl with the rainy-day eyes, and you could tell that she knew a thing or two about survival. There were wolves screaming in her, God how they screamed, and you could hear them in her voice when she spoke. She did not like to talk too much about how she felt, preferring to tell others to be good to themselves and hold their head high. I only wish she thought her scars were as beautiful as those she saw on others, but she didn't.

She was a lover of imperfections and thought the most beautiful souls were the ones who fucked up most in their lives, kind of like her I suppose. I had seen her pick herself up time and time again after taking life's beating, and when I thought she could not do it anymore she would say to me,

"I am the storm that made me, and there is nothing I enjoy more than the feeling of survival dripping from my fists."

Building Sandcastles

She built sandcastles out of the ashes she was
always rising from.
I knew she was tired of the flames others had left
her to burn in, but she would never stop.
She did it willingly for those she loved, and would
even hand them the match at times.
I saw her one day walking down the road with her
headphones on, I could see her scars that resembled
angels, and her tattoos that were her story.
She saw me, smiled, and took out her headphones
and said,

"I saw the sun rise today, and I thought to myself,
I am the inferno, and if I must burn to feel alive,
so, then I must burn."

Sometimes

Sometimes, I am on the brink of solving the mysteries of the universe, and other times I don't even know what day it is.

✧ ◊★·★◊ ✧ ◊★·★◊ ✧

Defector

I am a defector in the realm of society.
Black sheep call me mother,
and wolves call me sister.
I cannot contain who I am:
reform, conform, fit in, are no longer part of my vocabulary.
Accept me, reject me, both are welcome with open arms.

Thank You

To those that have betrayed me,
I thank you.
You have fed my wolves well.

She Keeps Her Circle Small

She keeps her circle small for a reason, even if it means
not letting those she loves, get too close to her.
To her, attachment is a liability, and she no longer kneels
to that master.

She would do anything, give anything to those she called
her friends, but if you should cross her, she will rip you out
of her soul with no remorse.

Heaven might have named her, but hell taught her how
to survive on her own.

I Am the Lonely Road

I am the lonely road,
untraveled by love,
followed by no one,
needed only by the path beneath me.
Its cracks won't break me,
its lines won't leave me,
and it beckons me to a place
that I can call home.

✧ ◊★ · ★◊ ✧ ◊★ · ★◊ ✧

White Noise and Dark Silence

I am white noise and dark silence,
chaos and harmony.
A twisted soul of fire and ice,
love and enmity.
I am the war against myself,
and peace for those around me.

Still Danced

She still danced in the mirror, smiling, and laughing as if nothing
in this world had hurt her.
There was so much life in her, there was death too, and it had taken
up residency in a dark and dusty corner of her soul.
The dark barely survived a girl like her, you would think it would be
the other way around.
She used to say,

"I am an empath with a filthy mouth and dirty mind. This world is done
fucking me for free."

You may not believe in heaven, but I assure you, one look in her eyes
and you will believe in hell.

The Last Fallen Angel

She did not carry pain like most people, she painted it into
colorful murals, and hung them in the foyer of her soul.
I often imagined her sitting on a black, tufted leather stool in a room
filled with empty easels, and pallets full of every shade
of hope and heartache.

She said love was her undoing, a nemesis that she had battled
for as long as she could remember.

It was not in her nature to turn her back on those she loved,
even when they had forgotten that she might need someone
too.

She never considered herself weak because of this, believing
that she was the last fallen angel, carrying her sword and sin
in each hand with pride.

I had not seen her in quite some time and happened upon
her on a not so sunny day.

I asked her where she had been, and she said to me,

"I have been with the night because it loves me more than the day."

How Heaven Was Named

She did not care too much about fancy things, new things,
or things that did not have enough soul.
She preferred dusty things, old things,
and things that had too much soul.
I believe it was because those things reminded her of herself.
The last time I saw her, I regrettably looked into her eyes,
eyes so dark and deep, that I swear that I could see how hell began,
and how heaven was named.

✦ ◊★ · ★◊ ✦ ◊★ · ★◊ ✦

Seduced By the Shadows

Some people attract the light,
but as for me, I am seduced by the shadows.
My soul is perpetually drawn to the lonely, abandoned, lost,
sad, broken, and hopeless.
I no longer know if I am the hunter or the prey
of those that lurk behind the love that I so desperately covet.
For I have willingly served them my heart on a silver platter.

She Had a Look to Her

She had a look to her like life didn't quite know what to do about her, and she didn't quite know what to do with life.

She could tell you a thing or two about it though, like how it can make you bleed sadness from your bones and pick slivers of broken dreams from your soul.

She wouldn't though, but would rather ask you about your day.

I do remember her talking about love once when someone asked her what it was like, she said "for me, it was base jumping without a parachute, while they wore theirs."

✧ ◇★ · ★◇ ✧ ◇★ · ★◇ ✧

Tested In Fire

This year my soul was tested in fire, and my heart broke in places I never knew existed. I had words left unspoken that turned to dust before they could escape my lips. I cried a thousand tears and dammed a thousand more. I will begin again whole; half white light and half black nightfall, and I will survive a new year.

Background Music

They told me I should try and fit in, not make any waves.
I told them to put on some background music
because I was about to fuck some shit up.

Wore Her Nightmares

She did not like to talk too much about her past,
for she feared her ghosts might hear her talking.
She did like to listen though
and be there for those who were haunted,
never asking them for anything in return.
I often wondered
if the world knew how she wore her nightmares with grace,
and that when she smiled you could catch a glimpse of the destruction
in her eyes.

Opens Up Her Soul

When she is distant, she is searching for the pieces of herself that were strewn amongst the universe.

When she is quiet, she is protecting you from the rage that has made its home within her.

When she allows herself to feel too much, she is trying to break down the walls that she had so carefully built, and when she opens her soul up to you, be a good human, and show her that you have a soul too.

✧ ◊★ · ★◊ ✧ ◊★ · ★◊ ✧

She Would Disappear

She would disappear into the forest of her soul when the world got too loud, never talking about those times, as if that was between her and her demons.

Her taste in music was just like her soul; wild, deep, and too much for most people to handle. She loved to rendezvous with the moon, telling each other secrets as they picked stardust out of their darkness.

Heaven Hiding In Me

She would get intoxicated by the moon and would ramble on about how she was an orphan of the stars.

"I saw heaven hiding within me," she would say, as she sipped on her darkness like her favorite summer drink.

She abandoned her demons long ago, claiming they only wanted her when she was weak, and she was far from that.

A queen of agony, a perfect storm, a woman bred for war, and she would proudly wear her scars like medals. What was a fire-breathing dragon, but the woman who would not allow the world to extinguish her flame.

Stardust and Unconditional Love

I have heard tales told about some souls that were forged out of
stardust and unconditional love.
Those souls were then placed inside babes who dreamt of angels
singing them lullabies within the wombs of their mothers.
Those babes would then grow up to learn the meaning of pain
and cruelty at the hands of the world and the people they love.
Yet, they will still love and love unconditionally.
Those souls will carry great burdens, burdens most would not
understand, and never experience.
Yet, they still love,
even when the world has turned its back on them.
It is who they are, and loving others is the only thing that keeps
them alive when everything around them is falling apart.
They are the angel's breath, warriors until the end,
and it is they that will suffer and love the most.

Soulmates and Magic

She talked about soulmates and magic, dreams and destiny, and held onto each day as if it was her last.

The dark was just another word to her, and she became its only master, wielding hell in one hand and heaven in the other.

What was a beast but the girl who built her life on a mountain of heartache, and a pocket full of pain.

✧ ◇★ · ★◇ ✧ ◇★ · ★◇ ✧

The Beast

I could not defeat the beast that made my heart its home.
So, I became the beast,
and together we don't take shit from anyone.

Amongst a Beast

When asked how I lived in the company of monsters,
I said, "They did not know they too were amongst a beast."

That Bad Ass Man

It was when he broke that I finally understood what made him who he was. He has a good heart, no, he has a beautiful heart, which had been tortured and burned because he 'needed' to be loved.

A bad childhood, and adulterous lovers, created the beast that he had become. He doesn't take shit from anyone, and he had lost the ability to fear, well, he only had one fear, and that was to be alone.

That was his weakness, his demise, his self-destruction.
That badass man needed love, and he would destroy himself in the process of finding it.

Sunrise

It has been a long time since I have sat and waited for the sun to rise.
I love how it creeps out of darkness and paints the sky so fearlessly.
It reminds me of how I used to be.

Maybe, I have gotten too comfortable in the shadows, or maybe, I
have forgotten what it is like to feel alive.

So, here I sit, anticipating its arrival as if we are old friends that have not
seen each other in quite some time.

✧ ◊★ · ★◊ ✧ ◊★ · ★◊ ✧

Pages of My Life

What did you think he would find flipping through the pages of my life?
A saint, and not a sinner, angels instead of demons, love without regret?
My novel is non-fiction, not meant for the faint of heart.
If you wish to judge, please put me back on the shelf and let me live the
best way I know how.

Sunday Mornings

She spent Sunday mornings tip-toeing around her demons, picking up her pieces that they carelessly left lying around.

"Some things are better off left there, hiding beyond our shadows" she would say that as if it hurt her too to touch some memories in the daylight.

I wondered how such a loving creature could be so tormented.
I wondered why angels were allowed to fly too close to hell.
She always loved a little too much, a little too often to those who hurt her a little too much, a little too often, and she became her greatest apology.

I can't blame her for not liking to get too close to anyone that might make her feel, and I understood what it meant for her to do so.
She was made of simple things, like compassion and love, but with those things also came self-destruction, and God how she could make that look so beautiful.

The Moon and I

Untamed we are, the moon and I,
and my heart howls out to it
in a language that only it can understand;
guarding my dreams and fears
within its silhouettes,
away from judging eyes.

Free we are, the moon and I,
and it shines upon me in a way
that only I can understand.
So, I hide my love within myself,
away from deceitful hands.
Love that I would freely give
to another,
if only they were like
the moon and I.

Maybe It Was Love

It was three days coming,
and four nights going as the harpies sang,
and the angels' halos fell quietly to the ground.
It was four nights coming,
and three days going,
Maybe it was fear,
maybe it was fury
subsiding within me,
or maybe it was love.

✧ ◇★ · ★◇ ✧ ◇★ · ★◇ ✧

I Am the Lone Wolf

I am the lone wolf and the moon is my only friend, my lover.
No lies fall within its craters,
no deceit hides behind its shadows,
and on my darkest,
loneliest nights,
it is there for me,
reminding me that I am not alone.

Where Dragons Are Born

I have heard that dragons are born somewhere inside a child's soul, between their first star wished upon, and their last tear shed.

This Is Who I Am

I will never be your air-brushed magazine model.
I am unpolished.
I cannot be your network sex star.
I am exotic and erotic for personal viewing only.
I am not athletically fit.
I am sensually toned.
This is who I am.
If you love me, please do not instill insecurities
in me where none should reside.

✧ ◊★ · ★◊ ✧ ✧ ◊★ · ★◊ ✧

Grown Tired

She's not heartless you know, as some might think.
She has just grown tired of being discarded by those
she had been there for.

They Wanted Savage

She was the little girl playing hopscotch in the rain, the tomboy climbing from tree to tree, and she colored her rainbows in shades of gray.

Her soul was older than the oaks that stood watch over the wars of centuries past, and her flesh held the scent of honeysuckle drenched in battle.

She was the lady who played hide-and-seek with death, the woman who danced to the music of her own demons, and she painted her heart in hues of unwanted and forgotten.

She never let many people get too close to her, and allowed just a few to touch the chaos in her soul.

I think about one of the few times she had opened herself up to me, talking about the masks that people wear so well, saying

"They wanted savage, then flinched when I sunk my soul into theirs."

You Know Me?

You believe you know me, why is that? Have you consoled my demons, appealed to my angels, or delved into my soul? My appearance, my possessions, nor my past or present defines me. So, hold your condemning tongue for someone who gives a damn.

✧ ◊★ · ★◊ ✧ ◊★ · ★◊ ✧

Creep Into My Soul

I am not a reflection of your insecurities.
So, swallow your venomous opinions of my life.

I've devoured demons greater than you.
I've slept with the spirits of regret,
 befriended pain, and made heartache my lover.

So, come creep into my soul, and see if you can survive the night.

I think not.

The Other Girls

She said the other girls did not like her,

they said she was too dark,

and I told her this was not true.

The other girls feared her,

because she thought for herself, and she had no 'need' to

think like them or to fit in with what society considers 'beautiful'.

I told her that this makes her powerful,

      indestructible,

and that she will never break under the weight of the cruel world.

✧ ◇★ · ★◇ ✧ ◇★ · ★◇ ✧

Bed of Belladonnas

I held myself accountable for the hell that was created.

I knew I should have refused that dance with the devil;

leaving him there, where I found him,

perched on a bed of belladonnas.

To Be You

No one can feel what it is like to be you
What it is like for you to live, to die
To taste life in its sweetest
To taste life in its bitterness
Riding on the coattails of the dark rider
Holding your breath at sunset
Hoping to make it to sunrise
Keeping it together, letting it fall apart
Keeping it steady
When all you see is darkness
And you would rather not talk about it
Smiling as if everything is alright
Laughing as if it does not hurt to be you
You
The angel with bloody knuckles
Who has earned their wings

Armor

A knight in shining armor.
I never cared too much about that.
Now, a knight in battered armor
Well, that is another story.

Turn Loose Your Wolves

She kept to herself most of the time, and I suppose I couldn't blame her for that. It was not hard for her to make friends, it was actually easy if that is what she wanted.

She did not have many confidants, either for the lack of trust or because people just couldn't get her. She was not one to waste her time or breath trying to explain herself to those who view themselves as preachers of righteousness.

There were things she had been through, terrible things, and you could see her wars dripping from her fingertips. I think there was a part of her that enjoyed listening to others, she would rather take on their battles than give them her own. A soldier to the end.

She did talk sometimes about certain moments in her life that burned holes in her soul, and when she did it always sounded as if she was laughing. Like life had tried its best to break her, and the devil himself had no idea what to do with her.

I think back on a night kind of like this, it was a bit too dark, even for the darkness, and the clouds hung low with thunder looming inside of them. It was about to rain, you could smell it coming, and that is when I saw her standing out in the field with her head to the sky.

I wanted to go to her, but I didn't want to, because she would say things, things that would echo in my mind forever.

Lightning struck, and I ran out to her, heart racing, and fists clenched with anticipation. I stood next to her, and the rain began in a slow rhythmic tumble from the sky.

She did not turn to look at me, she kept her head tilted to the sky when she said

"Turn loose your wolves, and I will give them a home in me."

What Ever Happened to Sunshine

What ever happened to Sunshine? That is what they used to call her when she was a little girl because she giggled with the sun, as if it spoke to her in a way that only she could understand.

Butterflies and dandelion wishes kept her busy on most days. The days before the clouds came, and hid the sun away from her.

Sunshine met darkness, and they became inseparable.

She grew into a beautiful, but haunted soul, and no matter how much she gave, how much she loved, it always seemed as if storms and destruction followed her.

It made me sad to think that she knew of hell, but it made me smile to know that even hell was jealous of the fire that burned in her soul.

So, whatever happened to Sunshine, the little girl with dreams as big as her heart?

I believe she is still out there somewhere.

I miss her.

I hope that one day I will look in the mirror, and see her once again.

✧ ◊★ · ★◊ ✧ ◊★ · ★◊ ✧

ABOUT THE AUTHOR

Lisa Lilith grew up along the coast, with a great love of the ocean, the mountains, and words written from the soul.

She has been writing since she was a child-- plucking words from the shadows of her heart and soul, writing from dark places, and you will find her picnicking with pen and paper on the other side of the rainbow.

Lisa's work is not for the faint of heart, and does not sugar-coat life. She has tasted death and abuse, and believes life is bittersweet in its most harrowing moments.

For more of her work you can follow Lisa on Facebook at facebook.com/LLMusings

Lisa also has typed pieces of her work, as well as custom designed items available through Etsy at etsy.com/shop/LLMusingsMoonFreak

✧ ◇★ · ★◇ ✧ ◇★ · ★◇ ✧

If you have enjoyed this collection of poetry and prose from Lisa, please consider leaving a review on your website of choice.

Made in United States
Troutdale, OR
07/05/2023

11005062R00090